RICK SARKISIAN, PH.D.

Tools from Joseph's Workshop

Credits

Cover photo by Patrick Evangelho and Mullins Studio

The artist/creator of the wooden mantle clock featured on the cover is
Wayne Westphale of Contemporary Time, Inc.,
P.O. Box 4883, Steamboat Springs, CO 80477, (970) 879-4124

Cover and graphic design by Riz Marsella

Illustrations by Jim Goold

©2004 LifeWork Press
All rights reserved
ISBN 0-9743962-5-7
Library of Congress Control Number: 2004117253
Printed in the United States of America

DEDICATION

To St. Joseph, the chosen father of Jesus.

ACKNOWLEDGEMENTS

I am very grateful for the help, encouragement and editorial assistance of Father Larry Toschi, OSJ, Father Brian Crawford, OSJ, Mike Phillips, Christopher Knuffke, and my dear wife.

I am also thankful for my dad who introduced me to the world of tools at an early age and to our Lord, Jesus Christ, who provides me with the tools I need today as husband, father and friend.

Special mention needs to be made about the beautiful tool drawings seen throughout this book. They were created by master illustrator, Jim Goold. Just looking at them makes me want to go out and fix something.

TABLE OF CONTENTS

Part Three: The Mission

INTRODUCTION

*T*he next month of your life could be life-changing! Because over the next 30 days, you'll be shown the "tools" to strip away sin, smooth-out life's rough spots, build virtues into your daily walk and strengthen your spiritual grip. Tools given to us by God, and demonstrated masterfully by Joseph: the simple, humble craftsman God selected to raise His Son, Jesus.

Of course, no book can make that happen on its own. It takes desire and commitment on the part of the reader, too – the desire to change, and the commitment to make it happen. If you have that desire and commitment, here's how to get the most out of this book:

1] Watch *Joseph: The Man Closest To Christ* – the video companion to this book (see Appendix D for ordering information).
2] Read one chapter of this book every day for the next 30 days.
3] Challenge yourself to put these "tools" to work in your life, using the Shop Notes in each chapter to guide you.
4] Reflect on St. Joseph, prayerfully seeking his intercession and following his examples.
5] Pray for God to equip and encourage you in embracing these life-changing virtues.

I pray that the next month brings you personal growth and spiritual maturity like you've never experienced before. Go to Joseph, and let this quiet carpenter help you build a life that reflects the unique blueprint God has created just for you!

THE MAN

*I*n many books and works of art, Joseph is portrayed in such exalted terms that it's easy to forget that he was a very human, very simple carpenter from a small village in Palestine. A man who sweat and suffered and faced the same fears and problems we do. And while none of his words are recorded in Scripture, he has much to teach us through the way he lived his life, worked his trade and cared for his family. From his humble workshop, Joseph shows us how to use the powerful spiritual tools that help us become more and more like his son, Jesus. ∎

SAW

■ TOOL

Both hand and power saws have one basic function: to cut… to remove. To achieve that function, saws require sharp teeth and steady power. Joseph, the builder-craftsman, certainly knew very well how to cut wood. And Jesus knows how to cut sin from our lives, helping us with a "saw" having particularly sharp teeth to make those precision cuts in a powerful, skillfully-guided manner.

■ DESIGN

God removes sin with the "saw" of Sacramental confession, and His Son, Jesus, through His Church, makes the necessary cuts. We keep the saw teeth sharp by avoiding temptation and keeping our lives pointed in the direction of Jesus.

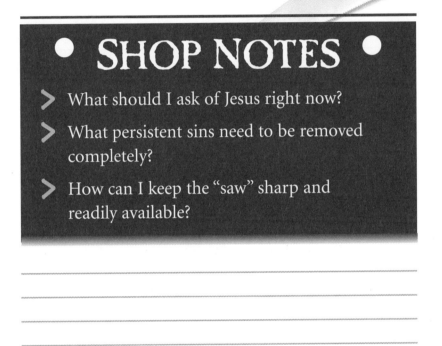

Slipping into temptation and sin dulls the saw's blade, and requires much more effort to cut out the sin.

● SHOP NOTES ●

> What should I ask of Jesus right now?

> What persistent sins need to be removed completely?

> How can I keep the "saw" sharp and readily available?

DAY 2

PUTTY KNIFE

■ TOOL

This versatile tool is mainly used to apply putty when filling or repairing surfaces, but it's also a handy scraper. It has a dual purpose: to repair and to remove. Similarly, Joseph worked patiently with wood surfaces in need of repair and finishing, and his son, Jesus, can help "repair" our imperfections and "remove" the rough spots that result from life's hurts, in order to help us gradually become "finished."

■ DESIGN

Like wood in the hands of the craftsman, we must patiently allow Jesus to smooth and finish the roughness in our life. He has divine putty (grace) which fills the nicks and holes left by sin. A rough piece of wood, apart from the craftsman, never gets finished. Our commitment to Christ means we place ourselves at Joseph's workbench so that his Son can work with us.

If we choose to remain in an unfinished state, then we make it easier for Satan to work his way into our life.

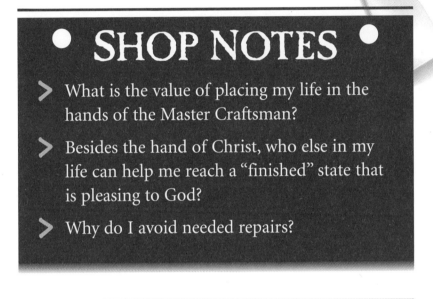

SHOP NOTES

> What is the value of placing my life in the hands of the Master Craftsman?

> Besides the hand of Christ, who else in my life can help me reach a "finished" state that is pleasing to God?

> Why do I avoid needed repairs?

MALLET

■ TOOL

The mallet is a blunt instrument usually constructed of wood, plastic or rawhide and comes in various sizes. While it looks something like a hammer, the mallet is better suited to driving wooden pegs than steel nails. No doubt Joseph taught Jesus how to select and use mallets in their work as carpenters. And now Joseph teaches us how to use the many "tools" his son gives us for getting through life.

■ DESIGN

It seems that Jesus has a unique set of tools (virtues and skills) for each of us, and He gives us those tools at precisely the times we need them. This is true not only for our personal needs, but also for the relationships in our lives. For example, as parents, each of our children requires very specific tools so that we can raise them properly, since each is different in needs, temperament and personality. We can ask Jesus for the tools we need to properly raise our children, and ask Joseph to show us how to use them.

"Use the right tool for the job." That was the motto of my high school shop classes. While Christ is always reliable in giving us the tools we need, Satan tries to give us other tools to accomplish his evil desires.

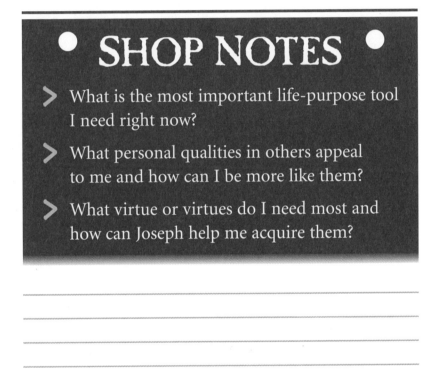

SHOP NOTES

> What is the most important life-purpose tool I need right now?

> What personal qualities in others appeal to me and how can I be more like them?

> What virtue or virtues do I need most and how can Joseph help me acquire them?

DAY 4

DRILL

■ TOOL

The drill is designed to bore holes accurately. To do this, the drill bit must be sharp and straight so that it can be guided with precision through the hole. Joseph guides us straight to Jesus, dependably and faithfully. And we can rely on Jesus for the grace we need to follow Him on the path to eternal life. To be good husbands, fathers and men of God.

■ DESIGN

The drill and bit work together to complete the task of boring holes. Joseph and Jesus had that kind of close relationship, and continue to work together in bringing the goodness of the Christian life into our hearts, minds and souls. We need a trustworthy guide like Joseph to lead us to the dependable truth of Christ for a life of real meaning and purpose.

Satan has other plans for us.

He wants to destroy any relationship we might have with Jesus, Mary, Joseph and anyone else who would guide us along the path to eternal life.

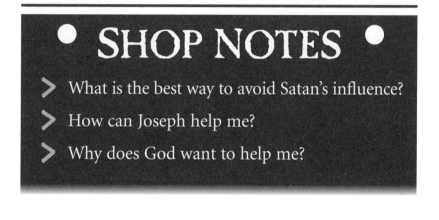

SHOP NOTES

> What is the best way to avoid Satan's influence?

> How can Joseph help me?

> Why does God want to help me?

RAKE

■ TOOL

The rake has individual tines that work together as one unified force. Like the tines of the rake, Joseph and Mary also worked together to help usher in the message of salvation through their son, Jesus. The Holy Family is comprised of three individuals united to give us a clear picture of God's plan for the family.

■ DESIGN

We are called to join Joseph, Mary and the Saints in sharing Christ with others. We are all "tines" on the "rake" of Christianity, working together to bring the lives of others – like leaves on the ground – into the heart of the Gospel message. As men, we can be particularly effective when we demonstrate a lively faith in our actions and words.

But there is another rake out there competing for souls: a demonic one, with tines of temptation, evil and sin. We must be ever-vigilant for it or we could be swept into hell.

● SHOP NOTES ●

> What is the most important function of the Christian "rake"?

> How can I more effectively join the Church community in spreading the message of salvation?

> In what ways can I avoid the "rake" of evil?

DAY **6**

PRUNING SHEARS

■ TOOL

Used to cut back vegetation, the pruning process often sacrifices living branches in order to promote long-term growth. Joseph knew that whatever sacrifices he made would contribute to the overall benefit of Jesus and Mary. Likewise, Jesus calls us to prune back behaviors, attitudes and lifestyle choices for our long-term spiritual benefit.

■ DESIGN

Orchards and vineyards are abundant in my home state of California, where trees and vines are regularly pruned so that greater yield will ultimately result. Jesus works in much the same way, pruning back various aspects of our lives so that we can grow ever closer to the person He wants us to become.

We must be on guard for the Enemy who wants to do much more than judicious pruning. Slowly but surely, he wants to sever us from the roots of faith that feed and nourish us. His ultimate goal is our complete separation from God.

● SHOP NOTES ●

> What is the value of pruning in the life of a Christian?

> What good aspects of my life need pruning for greater yield?

> What bad aspects need to be removed completely?

PLUMB BOB

■ TOOL

A suspended line weighted at one end, the plumb bob is always dependable, always showing true vertical, regardless of the situation. Joseph shows us how to remain centered on the Father's will and remain true to Jesus and Mary. Just as Joseph and Mary were centered on Christ, we are called to be centered on Christ who, in turn, depends on us to be a witness to others.

■ DESIGN

If we remain dependable and true to the Holy Family – Jesus, Mary and Joseph – we will have taken a big step along the path to eternal life. Joseph and Mary point us to Jesus, like a straight line between two points.

Satan wants to change our orientation; to become centered on the world and its allure. That's why life is a struggle. So hang in there!

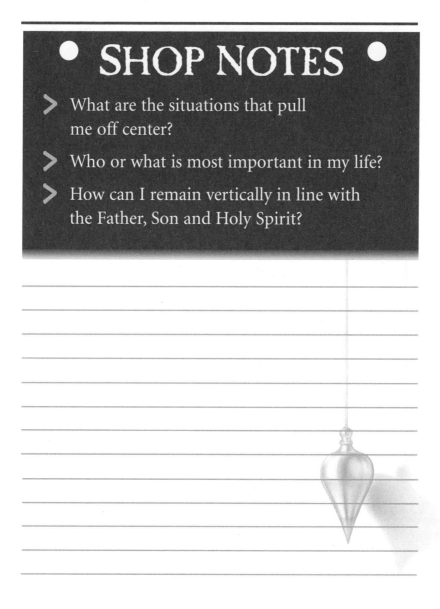

SHOP NOTES

> What are the situations that pull me off center?

> Who or what is most important in my life?

> How can I remain vertically in line with the Father, Son and Holy Spirit?

DAY 8

POCKETKNIFE

■ TOOL

The pocketknife is a handy little multi-faceted device.
(I like the kind with a blade, file, scissors, tweezers and a tooth-pick.) Joseph demonstrates the many gifts which God provided him. He was a craftsman who probably worked with wood, stone and other hard materials. But he was much more than that. He was also a man of God… a just man, a devoted husband and father. Like Joseph, we are called to use the gifts and talents God offers in His providence, becoming more and more a true follower of Christ.

■ DESIGN

Jesus equips us with the tools we need to fulfill the unique vocation and mission He gives to each of us. In the home, the workplace, church and society, we must daily rely on Christ to help us through the wide range of situations we might encounter. How do we use His tools?

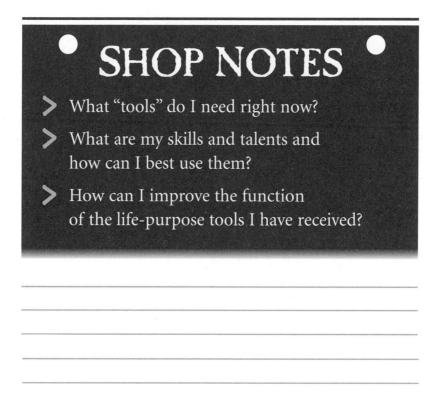

Joseph is certainly qualified to show us how. After all, he was a builder who taught his son to use the tools of his trade. Joseph is still a builder today. Not a builder of furniture, but a builder of lives.

Be aware: Satan has his own brand of tools, like lust, envy and pride... an ample supply for everyone.

SHOP NOTES

> What "tools" do I need right now?

> What are my skills and talents and how can I best use them?

> How can I improve the function of the life-purpose tools I have received?

JACK

■ TOOL

The jack is commonly used to elevate an automobile and bear its weight. Similarly, Joseph, as a spokesman for our needs, raises up our prayers to Jesus. And Christ gives us the strength to bear the weight of our burdens.

■ DESIGN

Each of us has our share of brokenness – being in need of repair, of healing. The passion of Christ, seen so vividly in the Stations of the Cross, is a reminder of how our sins were carried by the One who had no sin, and who will continue to bear our crosses today. Joseph transports our needs to the shoulders of Jesus. And the Holy Spirit will bring us comfort, sharing in our burdens and trials.

The secular worldview is that faith is a "crutch" for those too weak to handle things on their own, or too "unenlightened" in their humanistic self-empowerment. These are the kinds of views that Satan loves to promote, since they take us from Christ-centered to self-centered.

SHOP NOTES

> What burdens am I carrying?

> What should I ask of Joseph?

> How can Jesus help me?

DAY 10

PLIERS

■ TOOL

Pliers are amazing little devices – sort of like powerful extensions of our hands and fingers that enable us to securely grasp items that are beyond our reach. In his obedience to God's will, Joseph shows us clearly what it means to be an extension of God's plan of salvation. Likewise, we can "extend" our own capabilities and multiply the power of our efforts by allowing Jesus to help us as we conform to His will. This requires our willingness to trust Jesus and to be obedient to Him as Joseph was obedient to the Father.

■ DESIGN

In obedience to the Father's will, Joseph raised His Son and devoted himself to the service of Christ. God's design for our lives is similar – to obediently serve the interests of Jesus, to be extensions of His presence to those we encounter. Like pliers, we can do nothing apart from the hand that holds us.

How do you view your life? As a do-it-yourself project or as a cooperative venture with Christ? When you cooperate with Him, you allow His grace to make your actions more than just human actions. When you cooperate with Satan, you yield to temptation and sin.

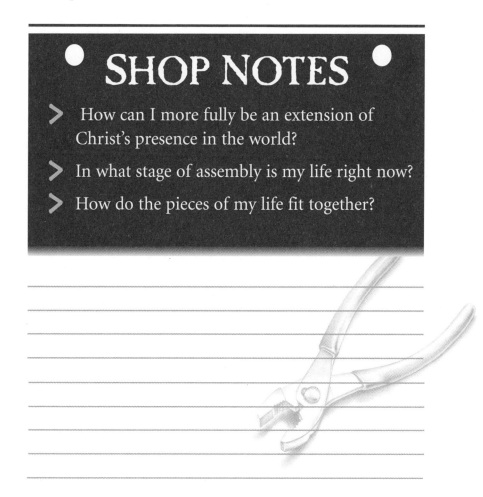

SHOP NOTES

> How can I more fully be an extension of Christ's presence in the world?

> In what stage of assembly is my life right now?

> How do the pieces of my life fit together?

THE CALL

From among all men on earth, God hand-selected Joseph for a very special purpose: to be the husband of Mary and the earthly father of Jesus. Likewise, God has a special vocation and mission for each of us – a one-of-a-kind blueprint for building a life of joy and fulfillment. Joseph shows us how to live out our vocations boldly and effectively, through his obedience, prayerfulness, faithfulness and love. He was truly a man after God's own heart. May that be our goal as well. ■

HOSE

■ TOOL

The garden hose is a channel that conveys water from a source (faucet) to a specific location (lawn). Likewise, Joseph humbly conveyed God's will to the world as husband of Mary and father to Jesus. As the source of all that is good, God often uses ordinary people to bring His supernatural grace into our lives. In the process, we can grow in holiness in the ordinary events that occur each day.

■ DESIGN

The Sacraments are often described as a channel of grace and indeed they are… connecting our lives with the abundant spiritual nourishment that is so vital in our journey to eternal life. In God's design, we are called and sent forth to fulfill a particular purpose in His plan of salvation. But we can't do it on our own. That's where divine grace comes in, allowing us to be strengthened for our mission… connecting with God through prayer, Scripture and the Sacraments. God is very accessible.

Avoid connections to the world that promise much but deliver little, like the quest for more pleasure, recognition and wealth. View your life as a personal vocation willed by God rather than a personal project.

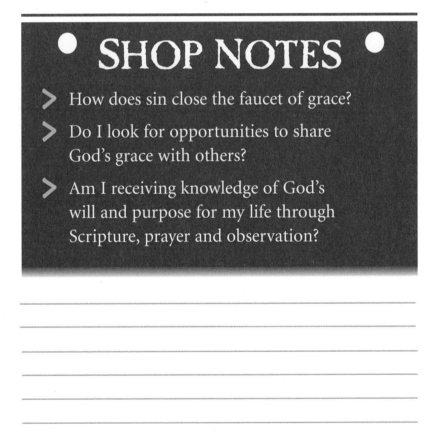

● SHOP NOTES ●

> How does sin close the faucet of grace?

> Do I look for opportunities to share God's grace with others?

> Am I receiving knowledge of God's will and purpose for my life through Scripture, prayer and observation?

DAY 12

CLAW HAMMER

■ TOOL

While the claw hammer has a twofold purpose – to drive nails and remove them – it is used more to bond than separate. Joseph's vocation presents a beautiful image of the inseparable bond of love he had with Jesus and Mary. Joseph seeks our permanent bond with Christ through his example of loving service and obedience.

■ DESIGN

As the claw hammer is used to bond two surfaces together, so, too, does Joseph show us how to bond with Christ. After

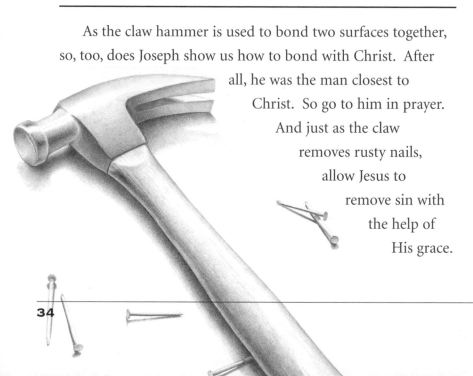

all, he was the man closest to Christ. So go to him in prayer. And just as the claw removes rusty nails, allow Jesus to remove sin with the help of His grace.

The rusty nails of sin are driven into our lives through the power of evil. If those nails are left in place, so is our bond with Satan.

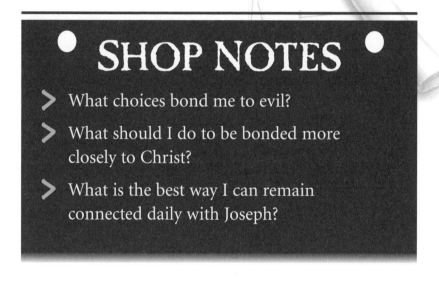

SHOP NOTES

> What choices bond me to evil?

> What should I do to be bonded more closely to Christ?

> What is the best way I can remain connected daily with Joseph?

CHISEL

■ TOOL

A chisel is useful for removing undesired wood in order to form a desired design. But it is useless without the hand that positions it and the driving force of a hammer or mallet that powers it. In his mission as Guardian of the Redeemer, Joseph's steady hand guided Jesus…just as he guards us and guides us to Jesus today. Like the chisel, Jesus removes sin so that we can fulfill God's design for us and grow in holiness.

■ DESIGN

Joseph is a most effective protector of all men, especially in our role as husbands and fathers. With Joseph aiding us in prayer, Christ removes evil from the influence of our life by the grace that flows from the Sacraments. Joseph, as "terror of demons," protects and guards us from the power of Satan.

Joseph is the hand that positions and guides us, while Jesus strikes a deadly blow against the forces of evil.

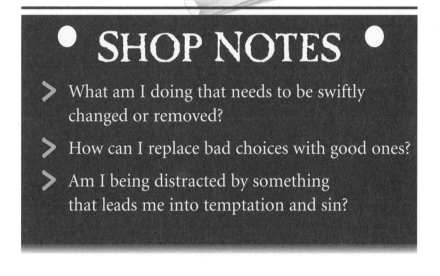

SHOP NOTES

> What am I doing that needs to be swiftly changed or removed?

> How can I replace bad choices with good ones?

> Am I being distracted by something that leads me into temptation and sin?

DAY 14

TAPE MEASURE

■ TOOL

A tape measure is a reliable instrument we can trust to give us accurate dimensions. Similarly, Joseph gives us a reference point for how we should live our lives as men in a manner consistent with God's blueprint for us. He is a superb example of authentic manhood. And the blueprint is found in the person of Jesus Christ.

■ DESIGN

God has a wonderful design for each of us. He is the Architect and, as members of His Church, we are His building project. When building anything, whether a small birdhouse or a full-size home, it is important to measure properly and follow the plan. Failure to do so results in uneven dimensions, and a final outcome that is unsightly, unreliable and inconsistent with the plan. That's why we need Joseph's help, aided by the reliable measures of Scripture, Church teaching and the Catechism. All to ensure that we are accurately engaged in the building process.

Of course, Satan has his own blueprint and measuring system filled with wrong dimensions and unreliable ways to measure them. Don't become his building project!

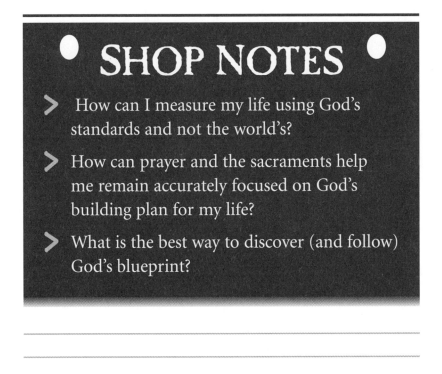

SHOP NOTES

> How can I measure my life using God's standards and not the world's?

> How can prayer and the sacraments help me remain accurately focused on God's building plan for my life?

> What is the best way to discover (and follow) God's blueprint?

CLAMP

■ TOOL

The clamp holds objects together inseparably until it is released. Joseph's trust joined him to God's will. Jesus, Mary and Joseph formed an "earthly trinity" that is forever known as the Holy Family – reflecting the Holy Trinity. Jesus offers a divine "joining together" that comes about through our baptism and submission to Him as Lord of our lives.

■ DESIGN

God offers us the freedom to choose between Him and the world. This is the choice between good and evil - between the free, cooperative partnership with Christ and the "clamp" of sin that Satan desires. Joseph's intercession, coupled with the power of Jesus, removes the clamp of sin and destroys it! We've got to trust Joseph to help us and open our hearts, minds and souls to the supernatural grace offered by Christ.

Once we fall into the bondage of habitual sin, then the powers of evil seek to keep us clamped more and more tightly to it. We need Sacramental healing to break free.

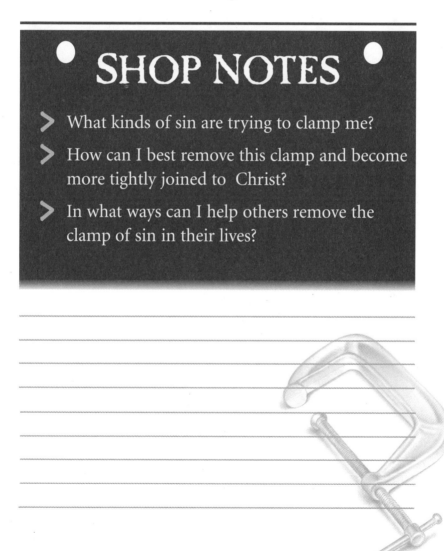

SHOP NOTES

> What kinds of sin are trying to clamp me?

> How can I best remove this clamp and become more tightly joined to Christ?

> In what ways can I help others remove the clamp of sin in their lives?

DAY **16**

SQUARE

■ TOOL

This precision instrument is indispensable for making sure surfaces are properly aligned so that they fit together accurately. Joseph's prayerfulness helped him to see how he fit into God's plan through marriage and fatherhood. He understood how God aligned him with Jesus and Mary. Now Jesus aligns us with the Father.

■ DESIGN

When we rely on Joseph, he leads us to rely on Jesus. And to rely on Jesus is to seek alignment with God. This means total surrender to a life guided by Jesus. By His grace, we become committed collaborators working with Him to bring glory to God on the path to eternal life.

Without Jesus, we are left to achieve alignment using our imperfect vision ("eyeballing"), and we are sure to fail. Every time we get out of "square" (God's will), we move closer to conformity with the world and further from the Kingdom.

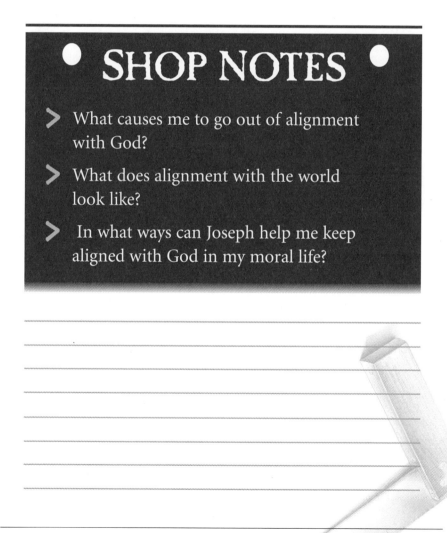

SHOP NOTES

> What causes me to go out of alignment with God?

> What does alignment with the world look like?

> In what ways can Joseph help me keep aligned with God in my moral life?

DAY **17**

BINOCULARS

■ TOOL

When it comes to bringing distant objects closer, no tool is more practical or effective than binoculars. They're highly portable, incredibly versatile and display precisely-focused, three-dimensional images. Through his faithfulness, Joseph embraced God's will and brought Jesus closer to us. Joseph continues to help us see Christ more sharply in focus. It's all about trust and surrender.

■ DESIGN

Through the gift of faith and a devout spiritual life, Christ's presence becomes closer, more real, more tangible to us. Joseph knows the joy that comes from a close relationship with Jesus, brought about by his trust in God's will. He wants us to experience the same joy in our life.

Satan tries to reverse our view so that Christ seems farther away, more like a "concept" than a real person – a great deception that we must avoid.

SHOP NOTES

> Who or what keeps Christ distant from me?

> How can I bring Him more sharply into focus?

> What is the best way to share the gift of faith?

DAY 18
WRENCH

■ TOOL

Each wrench is specially made to work with a specific nut or bolt. The fit must be perfect so that the wrench can properly secure a fastener. Joseph, hand picked by God, is a model of confidence and proper "fit" in living out God's unique vocation and mission within the Holy Family. And Jesus brings us true joy in living out God's unique plan for our life.

■ DESIGN

Wrenches are designed for tightening and loosening. Joseph, Mary and the Saints want to secure our lives more firmly to our Savior, Jesus Christ and will intercede on our behalf. In the process, their confidence in Christ becomes our confidence.

Satan, however, is eager to "loosen" our attachment to Jesus. He would rather have us attached to a life of evil and sin. If we are trapped by sin, we must seek the powerful aid of Joseph. He will ask Jesus for the tools we need to break the bondage of sin – especially impurity and selfishness – and reconnect us to Christ.

SHOP NOTES

> What are the forces that loosen my attachment to Christ?

> How can I tighten my relationship with Him?

> What does it mean to be joined to Christ?

THE MISSION

God gave Joseph an amazing responsibility – to lead, protect and provide for the Holy Family. Joseph's reaction? Quiet acceptance, instant obedience and unflagging faithfulness – a reaction worthy of our devotion. Yet Joseph, in his humility, deflects our attention away from himself and toward Jesus Christ, fulfilling another aspect of his unique mission. With Joseph as our example of authentic manhood, may we seek to be all that God wants us to be and do all that God wants us to do! ∎

DAY **19**

PAINTBRUSH

■ TOOL

Craftsmen and artists use the paintbrush as a tool for making surfaces more visually appealing, sometimes creating masterpieces as a result. Joseph's acceptance of God's will allowed himself to be touched by God's "paintbrush" in a special way, and became a beautiful image of God's paternity – an image we can see and appreciate to this day. God uses His divine paintbrush on the canvas of our lives, making each of us a unique portrait that reflects the nature of the Master Artist.

■ DESIGN

Created in the image and likeness of God, restored in Christ, we are part of one large tapestry that spans all time… all history. God, the Master Artist, renders each of us with the perfect colors, the perfect textures and the perfect frame for displaying the unique portraits of our lives… if we allow Him.

We fathers are often our children's first experience of God's Fatherly presence, making us very accountable for our words and actions.

Sometimes, though, we try to create "self-portraits" on our own, with colors, textures and frames of our own choosing. But we lack God's divine artistry. And the portraits we create can never be as complete or attractive as the one God wants to paint. These "self-portraits" fall short of the "masterpiece" we are to become.

● SHOP NOTES ●

> Am I creating my own self-portrait or letting God hold the brush?

> What image do I see right now on the canvas of my life?

> Have I "painted over" the sin and faults of my life by ignoring the need to change?

DAY 20
SCREWDRIVER

■ TOOL

Designed for the simple task of installing and removing screws, the screwdriver takes many forms based on a variety of screw types. Joseph, in his role as guardian and protector, took on a variety of challenges, and drew upon many virtues and gifts, such as confidence, hope and integrity. By faith, he lived out his vocation and mission in exactly the way God intended. He knew dangers existed apart from God's plan, and remained steadfast in his commitment to following that plan. It's called trust.

■ DESIGN

One of the greatest challenges, which also promises great excitement and joy, is to discover God's plan and trust in it. To hear His call and respond to it in faith, with the help of His grace. His call is a dynamic, unfolding process that allows us to freshly see how Christ is always present… always interested… always attentive to who we are now and who we are becoming. The choice is to live our way or God's way. Joseph is the perfect role model and teacher for helping us live God's way. He teaches us in silence and shows us how to be silent so that the Holy Spirit can fill our heart, mind and soul with God's will.

Satan knows that noise, static and interference can keep us from clearly hearing God's call. He makes these distractions powerfully present in such worldly snares as materialism, wealth-building and pleasure-seeking.

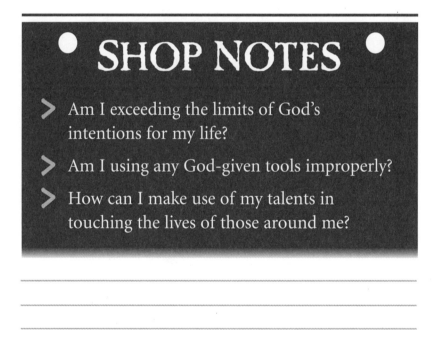

SHOP NOTES

> Am I exceeding the limits of God's intentions for my life?

> Am I using any God-given tools improperly?

> How can I make use of my talents in touching the lives of those around me?

DAY 21

FLASHLIGHT

■ TOOL

The flashlight exists for the sole purpose of illumination. Charged batteries are essential to its function – without them, the flashlight remains dark and useless. Joseph lovingly shows us the Light of the World, Jesus Christ, whose light pierces through the darkness more brightly than any flashlight. And when we receive His light – the light of divine Truth – we are also called to reflect it to the world around us.

■ DESIGN

In order to reflect the light of Truth, we must keep ourselves adequately "charged." We do this by living the Sacramental life, through prayer and Scripture, and through good spiritual books, media and friends. The friendships we develop with other men of God can help us be spiritually energized for the purpose God intended for our lives.

Stay away from Church, the Sacraments and God's Word, and you'll be far removed from the supernatural power of His grace.

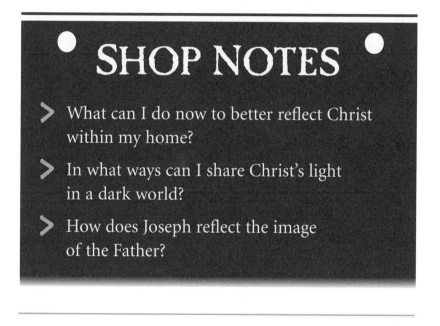

SHOP NOTES

> What can I do now to better reflect Christ within my home?

> In what ways can I share Christ's light in a dark world?

> How does Joseph reflect the image of the Father?

DAY 22

SHOVEL

■ TOOL

A shovel helps us change the landscape around us - move dirt, dig holes, remove plants, and make piles. Joseph's life was a pattern of patience no matter how his circumstances changed. Through his Son, Jesus, we can (and should) pray for an increase in patience to change the landscape of our lives in powerful new ways, so that we can respond in ways that please Him. This may take time – God's time – and will require our patient hope and trust in Him.

■ DESIGN

Jesus is always interested in how we are getting along in our struggle for holiness. If we consider our lives right now, what does the landscape look like? Is it lush, thriving and bearing fruit? Or is it a desolate field of weeds? It's probably a little of both. If our landscape needs improvement, Jesus has the tools of patience, prudence and persistence for changing it, and Joseph will show us how to use them.

If we want to remove the "weeds" in our lives, we need the power of Christ to do it right. More than just scraping the weeds from the surface of our behavior, He'll rip them out, roots and all!

SHOP NOTES

> What are the weeds (habitual sins) in my life?

> How can Jesus help me rip them out by the roots?

> How can Joseph help me to grow in holiness, and to avoid temptation and sin?

DAY **23**

SANDING BLOCK

■ TOOL

A simple block of wood wrapped with sandpaper can effectively change a rough surface into a smooth one. Joseph, through his powerful intercession, will ask Jesus to smooth and shape us into the people God wants us to be. And just as sanding may require starting with a coarse grit and moving progressively to a finer texture, Jesus sometimes works aggressively at first to get our lives in shape, then follows with finer smoothing to help us become more like him. Joseph will remain by our side in the process.

■ DESIGN

Our lives begin as a rough piece of wood that needs shaping and smoothing. Just as Joseph taught Jesus how to finish a raw piece of wood, so too can he instruct us in the way to follow his son. Just ask for his help.

If roughness represents sin and smoothness represents holiness, then we need to ask Christ to "sand" us properly so that we can conform to the blueprint He has outlined for us.

SHOP NOTES

> What kind of "sandpaper" does my life need right now - coarse, medium or fine?

> What life-choices cause an otherwise "smooth" finish to be rough?

> How can Joseph help me progress from rough to smoother to smoothest?

DAY 24

GLOVES

■ TOOL

Gloves protect our hands from injury and often increase our gripping power. They both protect and strengthen. Joseph's virtues – especially those of humility, simplicity, obedience and purity - protect us from spiritual harm and strengthen our lives. With the help of God's grace, we can grow in the practice of these key virtues.

■ DESIGN

God has given us many tools that protect us from temptation and sin, and strengthen our spiritual "grip." Key among those tools is the large Christian family known as the Communion of Saints – holy men and women who are eager to pray for our intentions and needs. They will help us strengthen our grip on the person of Jesus Christ. They are models of the virtuous life we are to seek.

We need a firm grip on Christ to counter the grip of evil. The more we hold on to our Savior, Jesus, the weaker Satan's grip becomes.

SHOP NOTES

> What grip does Satan have on me?

> How can I break free from sin and securely hold on to Christ?

> Which virtues are most important to me?

FILE

■ TOOL

The file is designed to
smooth the rough surfaces of metal
or wood, and is usually applied before
sandpaper or steel wool. Joseph teaches us to
live a virtuous life, trusting in God's power to change
the rough "surface" of our lives, enabling us to be renewed in
deeply spiritual ways. He does this by seeking the intervention
of his son, Jesus, who renews us through an increase in the
Christian virtues.

■ DESIGN

Our course in life is guided by our inner beliefs, spiritual
gifts and the presence of virtues and vices. The interaction of
virtues and vices tends to rise to the surface of our lives, influ-
encing our actions in highly visible ways. To change from the
"inside out," we must let Joseph teach us the moral strength
found in the virtuous life. Approach Joseph with an open heart
and an apprentice's eagerness to learn.

In Satan's realm, there's a lot he wants to teach us about vices as part of his constant opposition to all that is good and holy. He is completely antagonistic to a life of virtue and moral excellence.

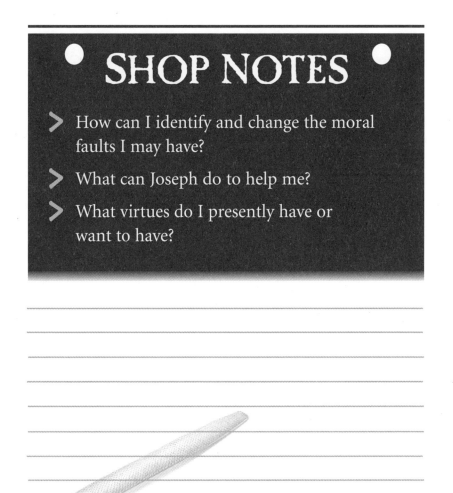

SHOP NOTES

> How can I identify and change the moral faults I may have?

> What can Joseph do to help me?

> What virtues do I presently have or want to have?

DAY 26

PLANE

■ TOOL

The plane shaves away wood to ensure a good fit before assembly. And the virtue of humility helps us "fit" into God's personal plan for our life. Joseph's humility is seen in his willingness to surrender to God's will. There was no pride in doing this. To conform to the image and likeness of Christ is to conform to His will.

■ DESIGN

The opposite of humility is pride – love of self - a vice that keeps us from embracing all that God wants us to be and do with our lives. If our lives are focused on self – that is, on power, pleasure, prestige and possessions – then we are filled with pride. But Joseph's focus was on serving God, and on the interests of Jesus. Joseph will help us be at the service of Christ and, in the process, become more Christ-like. Go to Joseph in prayer, asking for an increase in the virtue of humility.

Pride is one of the most pervasive and universal of human vices. It comes in many colors, like self-centeredness, self-importance, self-promotion and self-indulgence. The antidote is humility. Seek it daily.

SHOP NOTES

> What prideful behavior do I need to change?

> What does humility mean to me?

> How can I conform more closely to God's will?

HOE

■ TOOL

The hoe can dig into soil and cut down weeds while you remain standing. In effect, it does the "dirty work" so you don't have to get down on your hands and knees. If the landscape of our lives is blighted by the dirt and weeds of Satan, then we are living in impurity. Joseph shows us how to live chastely with purity of body, mind and spirit. We collaborate with Jesus in the process as we seek to sanctify all aspects of our life.

■ DESIGN

In conversation (prayer) with Jesus, we will gain knowledge of His plan for the landscape of our lives; learning who we are to be and what we are to do as men of faith. It is a landscape filled with thriving greenery and abundant fruit.

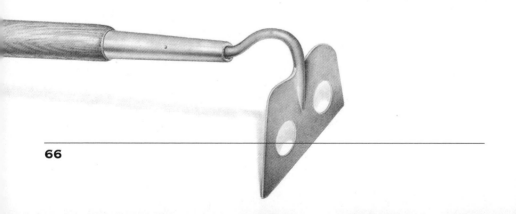

When we yield to temptation and delve into sin, we feed and nourish the "weeds" in our lives and encourage their growth, departing sharply from Jesus' plan. When the weeds of evil crop up, they must be uprooted completely; otherwise, the evil rooted in our life will continue to grow. That's where Joseph's prayers and Jesus' healing grace come in.

SHOP NOTES

> What are the "weeds" in my life and how deep are their roots?

> What am I doing to nourish them?

> How can I change the landscape of my life with Christ's help, so He can replace sin with grace?

DAY **28**

CENTER PUNCH

■ TOOL

The center punch has many purposes, not the least of which is to create a point that accurately positions a drill bit and keeps it from straying or "dancing" off the mark. Sometimes we need help to get properly positioned and pointed in the right direction. Joseph, as loyal man of faith, shows us how to remain faithful to our Father. It is a simple matter of following Christ…of surrendering our life to Him. A simple "yes".

■ DESIGN

Jesus Christ, Son of the Living God, is at the heart of the salvation message. In order to target our energies and life-purpose toward Him, we must ensure that we are centered in His Truth because He is the way, the truth and the life. There is no truth more accurate or dependable than that.

We must be ever-vigilant for false "truths" served up daily by the world's emphasis on self-pleasure, self-empowerment, self-enlightenment and self-enrichment.

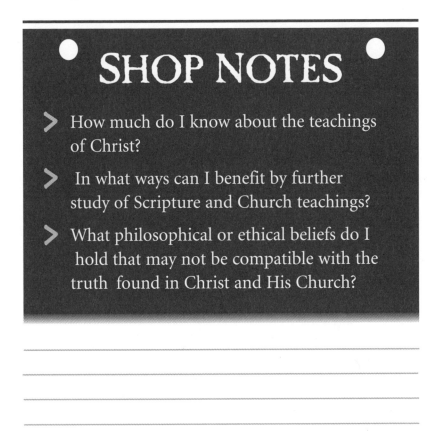

SHOP NOTES

> How much do I know about the teachings of Christ?

> In what ways can I benefit by further study of Scripture and Church teachings?

> What philosophical or ethical beliefs do I hold that may not be compatible with the truth found in Christ and His Church?

DAY 29

BACKPACK

■ TOOL

The backpack is designed to help us bear our burdens (literally!) whether we are toting books, camping gear or travel items. It is an essential tool for long hikes. Joseph, in poverty and hardship, carried many burdens, yet illustrates his patient trust in God to meet all the needs of the Holy Family. As the man closer to Jesus than any other man, we can go to him in our burdens, needs and brokenness. He will show us the Son. And Jesus will always be there to bear our burdens.

■ DESIGN

Joseph was called to serve the interests of Jesus – a mission he continues today. Such a purpose can make a deep impact on our lives if we invite Joseph into our pain, sufferings, confusion and difficulties. He will lead us to Jesus and Mary. And Jesus shows us how to patiently carry our burdens until we arrive at our ultimate destination: Heaven.

Jesus, Mary and Joseph walk alongside us in our brokenness. They are there to give hope and encouragement, even affirmation, while the Enemy launches volleys of worry, anxiety and despair.

SHOP NOTES

> What are the burdens I'm carrying right now?

> How can Jesus, Mary and Joseph help me with them?

> What burdens did Joseph carry in the Holy Family and how did he handle them?

DAY **30**

COMPASS

■ TOOL

The compass reliably points to north, and helps us gain a true sense of direction when we are lost. Joseph and Mary are witnesses of the "true north" found in the person of Jesus Christ. They never fail to direct our attention to their son. When we follow Joseph, Mary and the Saints, we gain a true sense of direction because we are led to Christ and the path to eternal life.

■ DESIGN

The Communion of Saints – all the holy men and women that have preceded us – are like individual compasses, each

pointing us toward Christ and eternal life with the Father. They are reliable and ready to help us on our earthly pilgrimage to Heaven and to guide us in making adjustments along the way.

The Saints are there to protect us from the magnetic attraction of Satan who wants to pull us off course, and to make us believe that some other direction is the better way to go.

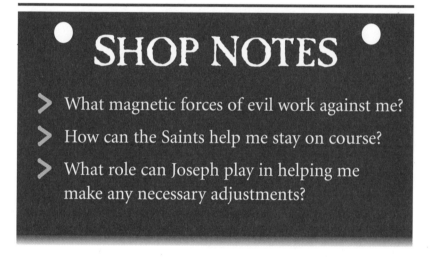

SHOP NOTES

> What magnetic forces of evil work against me?

> How can the Saints help me stay on course?

> What role can Joseph play in helping me make any necessary adjustments?

CONCLUSION

So…how was your month? I pray it was a month filled with tremendous growth, as you were introduced to the "tools" for living a more fulfilling and Christ-like life. But tools are only effective when you use them – after all, a chest full of shiny, unblemished tools may look impressive, but they're utterly useless in that condition. Tools aren't meant to sit in a box. They're meant to be used, to be put into practice, to prove their worth every day as they fulfill the tasks for which they were designed.

I pray that you have already begun to put these 30 tools to work in your life. Need a refresher on their various purposes? Look to Joseph, who showed Jesus how to work with the tools of his trade…and who shows us how to use the tools of virtue and authentic manhood.

And for continuing your spiritual journey, recording the insights along the way, consider using *The LifeWork Journal* (see Appendix D).

Thank you for spending the past 30 days training in Joseph's workshop. Now… let's get to work!

SCRIPTURAL REFERENCES TO ST. JOSEPH

Joseph mentioned by name:
Matthew 1:16, 18, 19, 20, 24; 2:13, 19.
Luke 1:27; 2:4, 16; 3:23; 4:22.
John 1:45; 6:42.

Titles of Betrothed, Husband and Wife applied to Joseph and Mary:
Matthew 1:16, 18, 19, 20, 24.
Luke 1:27; 2:5.

Titles of Parent, Father and Son applied to Joseph and Jesus:
Matthew 13:55.
Luke 2:27, 33, 41, 43, 48; 3:23; 4:22.
John 1:45; 6:42.

Joseph in relation to David:
Matthew 1:20 (1:1-17).
Luke 1:27; 2:4 (1:32, 69; 2:11; 3:23-31).

Joseph associated with Nazareth:
Matthew 2:23.
Luke 1:26; 2:4, 39, 51 (4:16-22).
John 1:45-46.

Justice and Obedience of Joseph:
Matthew 1:19, 24; 2:14, 21, 22.
Luke 2:4, 22-24, 39.

Joseph the Carpenter:
Matthew 13:55 (Mark 6:3).

Reprinted with permission from *Joseph in the New Testament*
by Fr. Larry Toschi, OSJ, pages 109-110. Available from *Guardian of the
Redeemer Publications*, 544 W. Cliff Dr., Santa Cruz, CA 95060-6147,
(831) 457-1868, toll free (866) MARELLO, www.osjoseph.org.

APPENDIX B

PRAYERS TO ST. JOSEPH

PRAYER OF POPE LEO XIII TO ST. JOSEPH
(TO BE SAID AFTER THE ROSARY)

To you, O Blessed Joseph, we come in our trials, and having asked the help of your most holy spouse, we confidently ask your patronage also. Through that Sacred bond of charity which united you to the Immaculate Virgin Mother of God and through the fatherly love with which you embraced the Child Jesus, we humbly beg you to look graciously upon the beloved inheritance which Jesus Christ purchased by his blood, and to aid us in our necessities with your power and strength.

O most provident guardian of the Holy Family, defend the chosen children of Jesus Christ. Most beloved father, dispel the evil of falsehood and sin. Our most mighty protector, graciously assist us from heaven in our struggle with the powers of darkness. And just as you once saved the Child Jesus from mortal danger, so now defend God's Holy Church from the snares of her enemies and from all adversity. Shield each one of us by your constant protection, so that, supported by your example and your help, we may be able to live a virtuous life, to die a holy death, and to obtain eternal happiness in heaven. **Amen.**

PRAYER OF PIUS X TO ST. JOSEPH THE WORKER

Glorious St. Joseph, model of all who work, obtain for me the grace to work conscientiously, putting the call of duty above my many sins; to work with gratitude and joy, considering it an honor to employ and develop, by my labor, the gifts received from God; to work with order, peace, moderation and patience, never recoiling before weariness or difficulties; to work, above all, with pure intention and detachment from self, having always before my eyes death and the account which I must then render of time lost, of talents wasted, of good omitted, and of vain complacency in success, so fatal to the work of God. All for Jesus, all through Mary, all in imitation of you, O patriarch Joseph. This shall be my motto in life and death. **Amen.**

ST. JOSEPH ROSARY

**May be prayed just as Marian rosary, substituting
the following prayer for the "Hail Mary":**
Joseph, son of David, and husband of Mary; we honor you,
guardian of the Redeemer, and we adore the child you named Jesus.
Saint Joseph, patron of the universal Church, pray for us, that like you,
we may live totally dedicated to the interests of the Savior.

Mysteries
1. Betrothal to Mary (Mt 1:18).
2. Annunciation to Joseph (Mt 1:19-21).
3. Birth and Naming of Jesus (Mt 1:22-25).
4. Flight to Egypt (Mt 2:13-15).
5. Hidden Life at Nazareth (Mt 2:23; Lk 2:51-52).

ST. JOSEPH NOVENA
OPENING PRAYER TO ST. JOSEPH FOR FAITH:

Blessed St. Joseph, heir of all the patriarchs, obtain for me this beautiful and precious virtue. Give me a lively faith, which is the foundation of all holiness, that faith without which no one can be pleasing to God. Obtain for me a faith that triumphs over all the temptations of the world and conquers human respect; a faith that cannot be shaken and that seeks God alone. In imitation of you, make me live by faith and submit my mind and heart to God, so that one day I may behold in Heaven what I now firmly believe on earth. **Amen**

Day One:

**The Annunciation
to the Betrothed Just Man**

First reading: Matthew 1:18-21
Second reading: John Paul II,
Redemptoris Custos, sections 2-3
One or more decades of the St. Joseph Rosary (prayed as Marian Rosary, substituting "Hail Mary" with "Joseph, Son of David"):

Joseph, son of David, and husband of Mary; we honor you, guardian of the Redeemer, and we adore the child you named Jesus. Saint Joseph, patron of the universal church, pray for us, that like you, we may live totally dedicated to the interests of the Savior.

Day Two:

Joseph Takes Mary His Wife

First reading: Matthew 1:24
Second reading: John Paul II,
Redemptoris Custos, section 20
One or more decades of the St. Joseph Rosary

Day Three:

The Birth and Naming of Jesus,
Son of David

First reading: Matthew 1:16, 25
Second reading: John Paul II,
Redemptoris Custos, sections 10, 12
One or more decades of the St. Joseph Rosary

Day Four:

The Presentation of Jesus,
According to the Law of the Lord

First reading: Luke 2:22-40
Second reading: John Paul II,
Redemptoris Custos, section 13
One or more decades of the St. Joseph Rosary

Day Five:

The Flight into Egypt

First reading: Matthew 2:13-15
Second reading: John Paul II,
Redemptoris Custos, section 14
One or more decades of the St. Joseph Rosary

Day Six:

The Finding in the Temple
and the Fatherhood of Joseph

First reading: Luke 2:41-52
Second reading: John Paul II,
Redemptoris Custos, section 8
One or more decades of the St. Joseph Rosary

Day Seven:

Joseph the Worker

First reading: Matthew 13:53-55a
Second reading: John Paul II,
Redemptoris Custos, sections 22, 24
One or more decades of the St. Joseph Rosary

Day Eight:

Patron of the Hidden
and Interior Life

First reading: Colossians 3:1-4
Second reading: John Paul II,
Redemptoris Custos, sections 25-27d
One or more decades of the St. Joseph Rosary

Day Nine:

Patron and Model of the Church

First reading: 1 Corinthians 12:12, 27
Second reading: John Paul II,
Redemptoris Custos, section 28, 30
One or more decades of the St. Joseph Rosary

Note: *Redemptoris Custos* is available
from Guardian of the Redeemer
Publications (831) 457-1868, toll
free (866) MARELLO,
www.osjoseph.org.

DAILY:

Lord, have mercy
    Lord, have mercy
Christ, have mercy
    Christ, have mercy
Lord, have mercy
    Lord, have mercy

God our Father in Heaven
> have mercy on us

God the Son, Redeemer of the world
> have mercy on us

God the Holy Spirit
> have mercy on us

Holy Trinity, one God
> have mercy on us

Holy Mary
> pray for us

Saint Joseph
> pray for us

Noble son of the House of David
> pray for us

Light of patriarchs
> pray for us

Husband of the Mother of God
> pray for us

Guardian of the Virgin
> pray for us

Foster father of the Son of God
> pray for us

Faithful guardian of Christ
> pray for us

Head of the holy family
> pray for us

Joseph, chaste and just
> pray for us

Joseph, prudent and brave
> pray for us

Joseph, obedient and loyal
> pray for us

Pattern of patience
> pray for us

Lover of poverty
> pray for us

Model of workers
> pray for us

Example to parents
> pray for us

Guardian of virgins
> pray for us

Pillar of family life
> pray for us

Comfort of the troubled
> pray for us

Hope of the sick
> pray for us

Patron of the dying
> pray for us

Terror of evil spirits
> pray for us

Protector of the Church
> pray for us

Lamb of God, you take
away the sins of the world
> have mercy on us

Lamb of God, you take
away the sins of the world
> have mercy on us

Lamb of God, you take
away the sins of the world
> have mercy on us

God made him master
of his household
> And put him in charge of all that he owned

Let us pray. God , in your infinite wisdom and love, you chose Joseph to be the husband of Mary, the mother of your Son. May we have the help of his prayers in heaven and enjoy his protection on earth. We ask this through Christ our Lord. Amen.

THE SEVEN SORROWS AND JOYS OF ST. JOSEPH

1. *Chaste Lover of Mary, how overwhelmed you were when you thought that you would have to end your betrothal to her. But when the angel of God came to you in a dream, you were filled with awe to realize that Mary would be your wife, and you would be the guardian of the Messiah.*
Help us St. Joseph, help our families and all our loved ones to overcome all sadness of heart and develop an absolute trust in God's goodness.

2. *Faithful guardian of Jesus, what a failure you thought you were when you could only provide a stable for the birth of the Holy Child. And then what a wonder it was when shepherds came to tell of angel choirs, and wise men came to adore the King of Kings.*
Through your example and prayers, help us St. Joseph and all we love to become like sinless mangers where the Savior of the world may be received with absolute love and respect.

3. *Tender-hearted Joseph, you too felt pain when the blood of Jesus was first shed at His circumcision. Yet how proud you were to be the one privileged to give the name of Jesus, Savior, to the very Son of God.*
Pray for us St. Joseph, that the Sacred blood of Christ, poured out for our salvation, may guard our families, so the Divine name of Jesus may be written in our hearts forever.

4. *Joseph, loving husband, how bewildered you were when Simeon spoke the words of warning that the hearts of Jesus and Mary would be pierced with sorrows. Yet his prediction that this would lead to the salvation of innumerable souls filled you with consolation.*
Help us, St. Joseph, to see with eyes of faith that even the sorrows and pains of those we deeply love can become the pathway to salvation and eternal life.

5. *Courageous protector of the Holy Family, how terrified you were when you had to make the sudden flight with Jesus and Mary to escape the treachery of King Herod and the cruelty of his soldiers. But when you reached Egypt, what satisfaction you had to know that the Savior of the world had come to replace the pagan idols.*
Teach us by your example, St. Joseph, to keep far from the false idols of earthly attractions, so that like you, we may be entirely devoted to the service of Jesus and Mary.

6. *Ever-obedient Joseph, you trustingly returned to Nazareth at God's command, in spite of your fear that King Herod's son might still be a threat to Jesus' life. Then what fatherly pride you had in seeing Jesus grow in wisdom and grace before God and men under your care.*
Show us St. Joseph, how to be free from all useless fear and worry, so we may enjoy the peace of a tranquil conscience, living safely with Jesus and Mary in our hearts.

7. *Dependable father and husband, how frantic you and Mary were when, through no fault of yours, you searched for three days to find Jesus. What incredible relief was yours when you found Him safe in the Temple of God.*
Help us St. Joseph, never to lose Jesus through the fault of our own sins. But if we should lose Him, lead us back with unwearied sorrow, until we find Him again; so that we, like you, may finally pass from this life, dying safely in the arms of Jesus and Mary.

> *And Jesus Himself, when He began his work, was about thirty years old being, as was supposed, the son of Joseph.*
>
> *Pray for us, holy Joseph.*
> That we may be made worthy of the promises of Christ.
>
> *Let us pray.*

Blessed St. Joseph, tender-hearted father, faithful guardian of Jesus, chaste spouse of the Mother of God, I pray and beseech you to offer to God the Father my praise to Him through his Divine Son, who died on the cross and rose again to give us sinners new life. Through the holy name of Jesus, pray with us that we may obtain from the eternal Father, the favor we ask…(Pause)… We have been unfaithful to the unfailing love of God the Father; beg of Jesus' mercy for us. Amid the splendors of God's loving presence, do not forget the sorrows of those who suffer, those who pray, those who weep. By your prayers and those of your most holy spouse, our Blessed Lady, may the love of Jesus answer our call of confident hope. **Amen.**

These prayers and others are from the *Family of St. Joseph Prayer Manual* (3rd edition), available from Guardian of the Redeemer Publications, 544 W. Cliff Dr., Santa Cruz, CA 95060-6147, (831) 457-1868, toll free (866) MARELLO, www.osjoseph.org.

THE OBLATES OF ST. JOSEPH

The Oblates of St. Joseph are a religious order of priests and brothers founded by St. Joseph Marello in 1878 in Italy. He was inspired to gather a group of young men who desired to consecrate themselves to the love and service of Jesus in imitation of the prayerful, humble and dedicated example of St. Joseph. St. Marello proposed a high ideal of an intense spiritual life united with a tremendous spirit of service. He viewed St. Joseph as a pathway to holiness in which we can become "extraordinary in ordinary things," keeping before us the image of the young Jesus – simple, poor and hidden away, working for our salvation through the toil of everyday life. Joseph Marello was canonized on November 25, 2001.

The Oblates of St. Joseph serve Jesus in whatever work is most necessary, without seeking to draw attention to themselves, working solely for the love of Christ. St. Marello desired that they remain open to whatever missions Divine Providence sends their way, particularly assisting local churches most in need, the Christian education of young people, and leading people to Christ through the example of St. Joseph. They began as a small community, but have gradually grown and spread.

In 1915, the Holy Father requested that the Oblates of St. Joseph start their apostolic services abroad, carrying devotion and the spirit of St. Joseph throughout the world. At present, they are working in the following countries:

Bolivia	Brazil	Nigeria	India	Italy
Mexico	Peru	Philippines	Poland	United States

The Oblates presently serve Christ through:

1. Loyalty to the Holy Father and the teachings of the Catholic Church
2. Spreading devotion to St. Joseph
3. Pastoral work in areas having lack of clergy
4. Christian formation and guidance of young people
5. Religious education
6. Catholic schools
7. Serving the elderly, immigrants and the poor
8. Spiritual direction for retreats
9. Foreign missions

Lay Associates

Associates to the Oblates of St. Joseph are lay men and women (and priests) without profession of vows, who choose to live a life of consecration to God and the Church in a spirit of collaboration with the Oblates. They take interest in the activities willed by St. Marello and share in the spiritual benefits, rendering service within or outside the Oblate communities under the direction of the superior.

As associates, they live the spirituality of St. Joseph according to the model of St. Marello, join with the Oblates in prayer, and work closely with the Oblates in a number of areas, including:

1. Youth ministry
2. Parish ministry
3. Vocation ministry
4. Social Apostolates
5. Missionary Apostolates
6. Spreading devotion to St. Joseph

The commitment to be a Lay Associate includes private consecration with promises to serve God in imitation of St. Joseph (humility, hidden life, hard work, union with Jesus). The preparation of an associate in the Oblates of St. Joseph will include learning to grow spiritually, active ministry and a life of prayer and service.

God's Call

It is the Lord who chooses and calls those whom he desires "… to follow more closely the Divine Master" (Saint Marello). To help discover these callings, men who feel called to join the Oblates of St. Joseph program as a priest or brother are encouraged to prayerfully consider the nature and purpose of their commitment.

If you would like more information about the Oblates of St. Joseph, please write to the Oblates of St. Joseph, 544 W. Cliff Dr., Santa Cruz, CA 95060-6147, call (831) 457-1868, or send an e-mail to provincial@osjoseph.org. Visit the Oblates of St. Joseph website at www.osjoseph.org.

PRAYER FOR VOCATIONS

Oh, Jesus, the Good Shepherd, when you saw your people abandoned like sheep without a shepherd you said, "The harvest is rich, but the laborers are scarce," and you urged us to pray to your heavenly Father to send workers to gather his harvest. Through the intercession of your most Holy Mother Mary, St. Joseph and all the Saints, graciously hear our prayer. Send to your church many workers filled with zeal for the salvation of souls. Grant our request by the most Precious Blood which you shed for us and by the merits of your Sacred Heart. **Amen.**

FROM THE LIFEWORK PRESS LIBRARY

JOSEPH: THE MAN CLOSEST TO CHRIST

The video companion to the book you're reading, *Joseph: The Man Closest To Christ* is a 65-minute presentation with insights and commentary from a variety of Catholic speakers and teachers. It explores all aspects of St. Joseph – the historical man, his response to God's call and the many ways in which he reflects the nature of God. *Joseph: The Man Closest To Christ* is available on VHS and DVD for just $19.95 plus tax and shipping.

NOT YOUR AVERAGE JOE:
The *Real* St. Joseph and
the Tools For *Real* Manhood
in the Home, the Church
and the World

by Rick Sarkisian, Ph.D.

This book is designed to present Joseph as he is and was – a rugged, hard-working man very much involved in the everyday life of his family and his world. A man with much to teach us about servanthood, integrity and authentic manhood. This book will help you learn to make Joseph part of your daily life, and embrace the virtues that make him anything but "your average Joe." *Not Your Average Joe* is available for just $12.95 plus tax and shipping.

THE LIFEWORK JOURNAL:
A Weekly Notebook
for the Story of Your Life
(Foreword by Rick Sarkisian, Ph.D.)

The LifeWork Journal is the 52-week notebook for tracking the spiritual growth, insights and discoveries in the "story" of your life. In addition to making journal entries, you will prepare a Personal Mission Statement, record key insights, reflect on a "virtue of the week" and track your spiritual growth week-by-week for a full year. *The LifeWork Journal* is available for just $12.95 plus tax and shipping.

These products are just part of the LifeWork Press library of life-purpose books and videos by Rick Sarkisian, Ph.D. Ask for a complete product brochure when you order!

To order, call Lifework Press
toll-free (888) 297-4300 or visit www.lifeworkpress.com